THE FINAL WEEK

A POETIC PRESENTATION OF THE EVENTS THAT OCCURRED IN THE LAST WEEK OF JESUS'S LIFE ON THIS EARTH.

CHIRADEEP PATRA

Copyright © Chiradeep Patra
All Rights Reserved.

To the One and only Lord God Almighty, my Saviour Jesus Christ, I humbly dedicate this book. May He be honoured and glorified through my musings on His passionate love journey as He headed to His crucifixion on the rugged Cross.

Contents

Foreword

I have known Chiradeep from his childhood as a thin gangly boy but it is only during the past few years that the manifold talents hidden underneath his quiet persona have come to the fore. He has not let physical infirmity deter him but has forged ahead multiplying the one talent into five and the five talents into ten for the Kingdom purpose. His indomitable spirit and passion for the Lord has drawn my admiration as has his way with the pen.

In this collection of eight short poems titled "The Final Week", Chiradeep has vividly captured the events that happened during the final week that Jesus spent on this earth starting from The Palm Sunday to His resurrection from the dead. No doubt we are all familiar with the Good Friday story but "The Final Week" actually transports us to the streets of Jerusalem as shouts of "Hosanna Hosanna" rend the air, to the temple bustling with pigeons and money changers, to the upper room to sit among the disciples as Jesus breaks bread, to Gethsemane to witness Judas' betrayal and then Peter's denial all the way to Calvary to see the Son of God dying on the cross as the representative and substitute for all mankind.

Amidst the hatred and evil scheming, Jesus stands tall: not as a victim of his circumstances but the Son of Almighty God deliberately fulfilling His Father's eternal plan and "Moving closer towards His mission". He was actually "Looking forward to the festival of Passover prepared to be the ultimate sacrifice - the slaughter". The irony of the situation will not be lost on the readers that "the delighted schemers and conspirators" "Agreed to buy the Son of God, the Redeemer in exchange of a mere thirty pieces of silver". With Jesus dead, all hope seemed lost. When He rose again breaking the chains of death, Jesus the Sun of Righteousness "tore apart the darkened sky", "bringing a new morning".

"*O Death, where is thy sting? O grave, where is thy victory? But thanks be to God, which giveth us the victory through our Lord Jesus Christ.*" (1Cor 15-55,57 KJV)

May this book be a blessing to all.

Sumita Das

Additional Secretary, Govt. of Odisha

Preface

Jesus Christ, the Saviour of the world lived a little over thirty three years on this earth before His crucifixion on the cross at Calvary, His glorious resurrection and His ascension to heaven. There were eight days of His life beginning with His triumphal entry into Jerusalem up to His resurrection that bear immense significance. This book, The Final Week is a poetic depiction of all the events that happened starting from Palm Sunday till Resurrection Sunday.

Acknowledgements

This book is a collection of poems written in reflection of Jesus' journey to His crucifixion and His triumph over death and sin. I humbly acknowledge the inspiration of the Holy Spirit behind encouraging me to compile my poems in the form of a book.

Human inspiration provides a tangible push to every work that we showcase. My all-time inspiration has been my own uncle, Samuel Patra. He is the star of the Patra family and words have been his forte. I feel privileged to have acquired the knack of writing like him, to a great extent. I am grateful to him for inspiring me so much.

I am grateful to Sumita Das, a busy Govt. official and a doting mother, who took out time for my book and gave her valuable inputs. She has written warmly of me and my work in her endorsement of this book. Thank you so much!

Word queen, Saakshi Gupta has always been very supportive all through these years of my writing - editing my works on the blog space that we commonly share. She is an excellent writer, who can literally write in any genre. I am thankful to her for extending her precious help towards this book.

The dynamic Pradita Kapahi, a fantastic writer with feathers of legal expertise in her kitty has been of immense help to me in the course of developing this book. I sincerely acknowledge the contribution of her ideas and suggestions for the improvement of this book.

I can't forget this person who is not only a good writer and poet but a believer who understands the scripture very well. Yeah, I acknowledge the invaluable efforts of Rajnandini Sahu for encouraging me to publish my writings and for editing the contents of this book after thorough proofreading.

I thank all my family members and friends far and wide who have always believed in my talent despite being aware of my ill health. Their fervent prayers and unflinching support have made me stand for the Lord and venture ahead to get this book published.

My heart is ever so grateful to God for giving me the idea to compile my poems into a book, for strengthening me in my weaknesses and motivating me all through the tough patches of life. This book is meant purely for His glory.

1. Palm Sunday

Hosanna! Hosanna! Hosanna!
The crowd sang and shouted Hosanna!

The King came riding on a colt
That gave everyone a big jolt.

An epitome of humility
He came to rule, reign and save the guilty
Carrying the banner of joy and peace
About to fulfil all prophecies.

Jesus made His triumphal entry
To stamp and seal His eternal victory.

Are you a captive of sinful bondage?
Or struggling with sickness, pain and sorrow?
Invite Him into your heart today,
Without sighing in vain for a better tomorrow.

2. Monday

God's temple was turned into a place of business,
That angered the Messiah, Christ Jesus.

'My father's house shall be a house of prayer,
How dare you make it a den of robbers?'

He warned them,
As He cleansed it with all authority.
Turning their tables and cleansing the dirt,
To bring back its sanctity.

Ask Him to take a look into your heart,
If it is filled with sin and corruption?
He will purify it completely,
With His eternal process of sanctification.

3. Tuesday

An eventful day,
He spent all the way,
With prophecies and parables
Lovingly teaching His disciples.

Amidst many questions and accusations,
Hurled at Him by the enemies,
All against His person,
His righteous and untainted deity.

Moving closer towards His mission
He listened to all yet remained quiet,
Neither did He lose His temper,
Nor did He live in fright.

He thus taught us plainly – 'How to stay focused',
Without being dismayed, only trusting in the Father God.

He explained the greatest commandment ever
To love God with whole heart and mind
And be responsible for the people around
Considering those as neighbours whom one daily finds.

4. Wednesday

The innocent lamb of God was anointed by a woman
At Bethany, in the house of Simon, the Leper.
Looking forward to the festival of Passover
Jesus prepared to be the ultimate sacrifice – the slaughter.

"What are you willing to give me
If to you, the Messiah be handed over?"
Asked he whom He gave a place so close and near,
Out of greed, turning into a ruthless betrayer.
The delighted schemers and conspirators
With all the happiness that they could experience ever
Agreed to buy the Son of God, the Redeemer
In exchange of a mere thirty pieces of silver.

The Lord knew everything but a word, He didn't utter
He was awaiting Judas to return, for He loved him like a
brother.

Are we stubborn and disdainful enough,
Not to come to Him with our humble petition?
Do we want to hurt Him like Judas
Or come running to Him with a heart of repentance?

5. Thursday

The greatest became the least
While having the Passover feast.

Teaching the disciples to be humble
The Master stooped down with a basin and a towel.

He set an example
by washing their feet
Commanding them to do unto one another,
the very same feat.

He revealed about the suffering
He would be going through
Without disclosing about the one
Ready with his venom to spew.

Soon, the devil took control of the betrayer,
The Lord telling him to quicken his heart's desire.

The garden of Gethsemane
became the place of preparation,
As the Son of man surrendered Himself
to be the ultimate propitiation.

Soaked with agonizing pain and sweat
Jesus asked His closest to pray and wait.

Alas! they never could overcome
their physical inabilities,
And share their Master's heavy burden –
His final responsibilities.

He prayed for all and for strength divine,
kneeling down at a distance,
Seeking His Father's will be fulfilled
without any resistance.

He suffered Peter's denial,
added to the pain of Judas' betrayal,
He bore the afflictions of all
as He became the sin portrayal.

Yet by all means, He displayed
the utmost love for them all
Leaving a lesson for us
about matters of the heavenly realm.

6. Good Friday

The first ray of the morning sun
Brought agonizing pain for God's Son.

He was dragged mercilessly
From this court to that
To be judged unjustly
Even when Pilate knew the truth in his heart.

Jesus was handed over to the ruthless soldiers
Who flogged the Saviour's flesh off His body.
But knowing His wounds will heal us all
He allowed the scourges, on Him to befall.

He walked the path bleeding till Calvary
Facing the humiliation of people's mockery.
He was tagged and treated as a criminal
And hanged on the Cross to meet His death final.

How do we know, how to even grasp
the torments of the Son of God!!!
The Holy Spirit departed from Him,
as He laid His life down for the whole world.

The thick veil of the temple was torn apart
At the gruesome death of the Saviour.
Jesus became the bridge between God and human
Paving the way for everyone a life forever.

He became sin
who had never known any sin
Yet He took the punishment Himself
to save me, you and all.

7. Saturday

The Messiah was crucified and dead,
The city of Jerusalem was blood-stained.

There was calmness all around,
All thought the chapter was closed to be forgotten.

While the disciples hid themselves
in the upper room,
The women who loved Him
got busy with rituals for His tomb.

The enemies were happy and rejoicing
Without any idea of what they had done and what was
awaiting.

The law of the Sabbath was kept, without the lawmaker
As all tried to go about their lives without the life-giver.

No one remembered,
what He had promised,
As nobody believed,
What about Him was prophesied.

8. Resurrection Sunday

Jesus, the Resurrected One
Broke the chains of death and its venomous sting,
Before the sun tore apart the darkened sky
Rising up on the east, bringing a new morning.

The bewildered women stood searching for His body
As the angels appeared to make their minds steady.

"Why do you look for the living among the dead?"
They said, as the women ran to let this news spread.

The disciples couldn't believe it
Until they saw Him face to face.

Fear encompassed the enemy camp
While His own rejoiced as He bridged the gap.

God justified mankind
by His message of the great salvation.
Jesus made it possible
by His death and resurrection.

Why On Earth Did Jesus Have To Die!

The death of Jesus Christ was the most horrific event of the human race. Those eight days of human history, on which I have written this book, are very painful from a human perspective. But there are certain questions that always make us wonder about these events. "Why on earth did He have to die? He is God. If He had simply used His might and authority everything would have come into order… Why then this high drama of such a painful death?"

It is important for us to understand the fact *why He had to die for you and me*.

God is Holy as the Bible says in Leviticus 11:44a, "*For I am the Lord your God. You must consecrate yourselves and be holy, because I am holy.*" God's attribute, **holiness** proclaims that *there is no relationship between holiness and unholiness.*

God is Righteous as well. The Bible says in Psalm 11:7, "*For the righteous Lord loves justice. The virtuous will see his face.*" God's **righteousness** announces that *there is no relationship between righteousness and unrighteousness.*

God is Just. The Psalmist says in Psalm 9:16, "*The Lord is known for his justice. The wicked are trapped by their own deeds.*" God's **justice** declares that *there is no relationship between justice and injustice.*

Man has sinned against God. Falling short of the glory of God he has become **unholy**, **unrighteous** and **unjust** as Romans 3:23 declares, "*For everyone has sinned; we all fall short of God's glorious standard.*"

All the above-mentioned attributes of God debar man from coming into the presence of God. General understanding says that the consequence of any wrongdoing is punishment. So, all men need to be punished. The punishment for man's wrongdoing is "DEATH", which we read in Romans

6:23, *"For the wages of sin is death, but the free gift of God is eternal life through Christ Jesus our Lord."*

But another attribute of **God is LOVE (includes kindness and goodness).** This explains His mind differently. Two Bible verses depict God's act of love vividly.

Genesis 1:27 says, *"So God created human beings in his own image. In the image of God he created them; male and female he created them."*

John 3:16 says, *"For this is how God loved the world: He gave his one and only Son, so that everyone who believes in him will not perish but have eternal life."*

God's **love** ensures and reflects God's heart - "I created these men and women in my own image. How then can I punish them? I will save them from this **eternal death**. I will make them **righteous**, **just** and **holy**. I will give them **eternal life**".

In this way, all men can ultimately come to the presence of a Holy, Righteous and Just God.

Therefore, the Bible says, *"So the Word became human and made His home among us. He was full of unfailing love and faithfulness. And we have seen his glory, the glory of the Father's one and only Son."* (John 1:14)

"Look! The virgin will conceive a child! She will give birth to a son, and they will call him Immanuel, which means 'God is with us.'" (Matthew 1: 23)

The angel who appeared to Mary (the mother of Jesus) told her, *"You will conceive and give birth to a son, and you are to call him Jesus."* (Luke 1:31)

Jesus is the name God took when He came in the form of a human and became flesh to take the punishment of man on Himself - to save us, to be an Emmanuel for us and to have fellowship with us forever and ever. ***On that cross, God showcased all His attributes together not even abandoning one.*** And so, He had to die.